What Does a CITIZEN Do?

What Does a Member of the Armed Forces Do?

Chris Townsend

Enslow Publishing
101 W. 23rd Street
Suite 240
New York, NY 10011
USA
enslow.com

Published in 2019 by Enslow Publishing, LLC.
101 W. 23rd Street, Suite 240, New York, NY 10011

Library of Congress Cataloging-in-Publication Data

Names: Townsend, Chris, author.
Title: What does a member of the Armed Forces do? / Chris Townsend.
Description: New York : Enslow, [2019] | Includes bibliographical references and index. | Audience: Grades 5–8.
Identifiers: LCCN 2017055224| ISBN 9780766098664 (library bound) | ISBN 9780766098671 (pbk.)
Subjects: LCSH: United States—Armed Forces—Vocational guidance—Juvenile literature.
Classification: LCC UB147 .T69 2018 | DDC 355.0023/73—dc23
LC record available at https://lccn.loc.gov/2017055224

Printed in the United States of America

To Our Readers: We have done our best to make sure all website addresses in this book were active and appropriate when we went to press. However, the author and the publisher have no control over and assume no liability for the material available on those websites or on any websites they may link to. Any comments or suggestions can be sent by email to customerservice@enslow.com.

Photo Credits: Cover, p. 1 Inti St Clair/Blend Images/Getty Images; p. 4 Stuart Monk/Shutterstock.com; pp. 8–9 Jewel Samad/AFP/GettyImages; pp. 10–11 STR/AFP/Getty Images; p. 13 U.S. Navy Photo/Alamy Stock Photo; p. 16 Library of Congress Prints and Photographs Division; pp. 18–19 Drew Angerer/Getty Images; pp. 20–21, 43 Scott Olson/Getty Images; pp. 24–25 PJF Military Collection/Alamy Stock Photo; pp. 28–29 Paula Bronstein/Getty Images; p. 31 Marco Di Lauro/Getty Images; pp. 32–33 Chris Hondros/Getty Images; p. 36 Sean Galbreath/U.S. Navy/Getty Images; p. 39 Smith Collection/Gado/Archive Photos/Getty Images; p. 41 Sandy Huffaker/Getty Images.

CONTENTS

Members of the armed forces come from across America, protecting the nation in various ways.

Introduction

Members of the armed forces come from all over the United States. These citizens choose to serve their country by fighting for it. Some are sailors on the high seas. Some fly airplanes. Others fight on the ground with tanks and guns. But there is much more to service than just fighting. This book looks at the civic responsibility of service where ordinary men and women sign up to defend their country. Not every citizen can serve. Those who do perform a very special role for their country.

The United States has had armed forces since before it was even a country! The US Army, Navy, Air Force, Marines, and Coast Guard are all part of the armed forces. While there are many who serve their country in government, these citizens are ready to take up weapons when needed and fight for their country or defend it.

No one is forced to serve in the armed forces. While there used to be a draft to make people join the military, today's service is made up of volunteers. Not everyone can join. Each service has its own education, age, and physical fitness requirements. A special test lets volunteers know what jobs they would be best at. Some jobs require a college degree.

Once new service members join, they have to be trained. First, they train to fight. They have to know how to defend themselves and fire a rifle. They also have to be in excellent shape. After basic training, every service member goes to school to learn a special skill. There are many different jobs in the armed forces. Every single one of them is important to the mission.

Members of the armed forces do not spend all their time at war. Most work normal jobs on bases here in the United States and all over the world. In the Navy, they take their office with them all over the world! In a lot of ways working for the armed forces is a lot like any other job. Sometimes that job is far away. Sometimes it is dangerous.

Of course, when there is trouble in the world, members of the armed forces can be sent to fight. Wars are uncommon, but even so there are a lot of other ways service members can help. They deploy all over the world to help after natural disasters or to defend those who cannot defend themselves.

Service means sacrifice. Sometimes members of the armed forces are wounded or die doing their jobs. Because they serve all over the world, often they have to be away from their families. The United States values members of the armed forces. The country cares for those wounded and honor those who have sacrificed for it. Service in the armed forces is challenging but can be very rewarding. Service members serve their country but they really serve all of us. They stand ready to fight so that others can live in peace.

1

United States Armed Forces

Citizens of the United States can serve in the armed forces. The armed forces defend the United States against enemies. All service members are volunteers. The US Army, Navy, Air Force, Marine Corps, and Coast Guard each are responsible for protecting one of the domains of warfare. The Army and Marine Corps primarily fight on land and beaches. The Navy controls the sea. The Coast Guard protects ports. The Air Force defends the skies. The members of the armed forces are called service members. Sometimes they are referred to by their branch of service. We call them soldiers, sailors, airmen, marines, and coastguardsmen, or coasties. Don't be confused by the word "men." The term refers to both men and women in the services. The president is the commander of all of the armed forces.

United States Army

The United States Army began as the Continental army on June 14, 1775. The Congress selected George Washington to be the

The US Air Force is one of the uniformed armed forces serving the country.

commander of the new force. The new army was made up of only infantry at first. Infantry is the main fighting force in the US Army. The infantry was originally made up of men with rifles. Women can join the infantry today. Congress then approved other branches for finance, supplies, engineers, artillery, and cavalry. The Army soon added other branches like communications, aviation, and Special Forces. There are many different specialties in the Army, everything from mechanics to heart surgeons.

The Army is made up of active duty soldiers, reserves, and the National Guard. Active duty soldiers work full-time. Most reservists work part-time and have civilian jobs. The National Guard is similar to the reserves but works for the state in which they live. All three can be deployed and spend time away from their families. There are over one million soldiers between the three types. The Army is responsible for fighting on land. There are some helicopters and boats as well.

United States Navy and Marine Corps

In October 1775, the Continental Congress directed the start of what would become the United States Navy.[1] The Navy's job is securing the seas. Securing the seas is essential to protect free trade around the globe. Today, the Navy has over four hundred thousand sailors split between active duty and reserves.[2] There are nearly three hundred ships in the Navy. The ships include all kinds, from aircraft carriers to hospital ships. The Navy also has many types of planes and helicopters. Sailors spend part of their time at home stations around the world and the rest of their time at sea. At sea, the Navy trains and conducts missions to support the nation's security.

The Marine Corps is the infantry of the Navy. They spend some time at sea. They also fight on the land and in the air. The Marines were the third of the original armed forces created by the Continental Congress in 1775 along with the Navy and the Army. There are just over two hundred thousand members.[3] Marines are known as "Devil Dogs" because of their fierceness in battle. The Marine Corps hymn recounts some of their

Created in 1775, the US Navy patrols the seas, with close to three hundred ships around the world.

Female Devil Dogs

Since the start, the Marine Corps has allowed only men to be in the infantry. The first female marine to join the Corps was Opha May Johnson in 1918. The marines hired her be a clerk.[4] In 2016, the military began to allow women to serve in combat jobs like the infantry. Women were quick to rise to the challenge. Now there are women marines who fight in the infantry as enlisted service members and officers. Soon, there will even be women special operators. Special operators are the most highly trained members of the armed forces.

earliest battles, including America's first battle on foreign shores in Tripoli, Libya. The Marines guard our embassies all over the world.

United States Air Force

The US Air Force began as part of the Army. In 1907, the Army Air Corps was formed to handle military operations with balloons and planes. Initially, aircraft were used to look at the battlefield from above. After World War II, the Air Force became the newest service. Since then, the Air Force has been involved in all aspects of air and space operations. Today, it also fights against hackers in cyberspace. There are nearly five hundred thousand airmen in today's Air Force.

Like the Army, a reserve and guard force make up about a third of that number.[5]

Most people think of planes when they think of the Air Force. The Air Force does much more than fly planes. Some get to fly spaceships! Many airmen don't fly at all. Most of the Air Force is actually made up of support personnel that help the flying mission. These airmen do everything from security to personnel management. The Air Force has bases all over the world. It helps all over the world

Col. Dawn Dunlop is just one of the many fighter pilots in the United States Air Force.

During World War II, recruitment posters encouraged young men to enlist in the military.

tell you about the services. They can explain what education you have to have before you can join. You must have a high school diploma or equivalent. You must also be eighteen, or seventeen with a parent's permission. After some paperwork, it's off to the military entrance processing station, or MEPS.

At the MEPS you have to take a test to see what jobs you would be good at. The test covers subjects like math and English. These subjects ensure your level of education. The most important score on the test looks only at these various English and math tests. There are also categories for electronics, engines, and shapes to see if you would be good at specific jobs. Once you pass the test, you have to be checked by a doctor. The doctor makes sure that you are healthy enough to serve. After passing the test and the physical, it's time to pick a job. There are hundreds of different jobs from which to choose. Some specialized jobs, like nuclear submarine mechanic, are offered in only one service. Other more general jobs, like mechanics, cooks, and administrators, exist in every service. Once you have picked a job and signed the contract it's off to basic training.

Officer Schools

Officers in the armed forces are responsible for leading service members and performing a variety of management and other specialized tasks. There are two types of officers in the armed forces. Commissioned officers hold command and advisory roles. Warrant officers are technical experts and pilots. Officers have a higher education requirement. Commissioned officers must have at least a bachelor's degree, and warrant officers must have at least an associate's degree.

Direct Commission

Sometimes, excellent enlisted service members are promoted to an officer rank without any college. In other cases, civilians with a special skill are commissioned as officers. This is called a direct commission. It is rare. Today, direct commissioning is mostly used for doctors, lawyers, and clergy. In times of war, a service member can earn a battlefield commission. Mostly, battlefield commissioning happens in times of war when there are not enough officers.[1] One of the most famous battlefield commissions was Audie Murphy, who went from being a sergeant to a lieutenant because of his heroism in World War II.

While some officers work in their degree field, many do not. A degree is important because officers must be good at thinking and must be excellent communicators. Officers are responsible for all of the equipment in the armed forces. Sometimes they are responsible for millions of dollars of equipment at a time. Some officers have advanced degrees like medical, legal, master's and even doctorate degrees. The armed forces have programs where officers are paid to go to more advanced schools in exchange for more time in the service.

Normally officers come through one of three programs. Some go to military academies like West Point and Annapolis. At military academies, students wear uniforms and have strict discipline requirements. It's like being in school and in the military at the same time. Others go to regular universities but take military classes along with their other classes. This is called the Reserve

Military academies prepare young men and women who want to join the armed services after graduation.

Officers' Training Corps (ROTC). Officers in the ROTC take extra training in the summer to get some practice in the field. Those who already have a degree or are enlisted with enough college credits can go to Officer Candidate School. Officer candidates with no prior service must go through basic training first so that they learn the basics of military service. Officer Candidate School is very tough. It has to be in order to create leaders in a few short months. It doesn't matter which path they choose, they are all equal officers in the armed forces.

Training

The first step of training for enlisted members of the armed forces is basic training. The various services have different names for this first school. The Army calls it basic combat training. The Navy and Marines refer to it as recruit training. The Air Force calls it basic military training. The Coast Guard calls its program basic training. Most people call this initial training by another name: boot camp! One reason is that recruits wear uniforms with boots for

All members of the armed forces must undergo rigorous basic training, challenging their strength and endurance.

most of the training. Basic training is tough physical training that teaches recruits the basics of their service. They learn to fight and shoot. They learn how to live in the field. They take many classes that every service member needs, like how to talk on radios using words for letters, like "alpha" for A, "bravo" for B, and "Charlie" for C. The training is hard but it gets service members ready to go fight in a war if necessary. Officers have a course, too, where they learn the basics about their new jobs.

After basic training, service members must learn a specific skill related to their job. They go to bases all over the United States. This is often referred to as advanced training. For those assigned to the infantry, advanced training is just like a more advanced version of basic training. Others go to schools to learn everything from dental hygiene to advanced satellite systems. This phase of training can last anywhere from a couple months to an entire year. At the end of training these new members of the armed forces go to their unit and begin performing their new jobs. In the next chapter, we'll look at the daily life of service members as they do their jobs.

3

Serving America

Working in the armed forces is like working any other job in many ways. The biggest difference is that sometimes that job is halfway around the world. Service members may also be called upon to do their jobs during war. It can be dangerous, which is why training never stops. Some service members do their jobs every single day while others only practice doing their jobs until there is a reason to fight. When there is no war, service members work their jobs and live their lives much like their civilian counterparts. Sometimes the only difference is a uniform!

Jobs

Some jobs are very service specific. The Navy has no use for tank drivers. The Army doesn't need submarine navigators. Every branch of the armed forces has pilots, though! You will also find cooks, mechanics, and personnel and finance specialists, as well as computer experts in every service. Some jobs have to be done

There are many different jobs available in the military, not just those involving combat.

twenty-four hours a day, seven days a week all over the world. These are critical jobs like medicine and air traffic control. Other jobs work a more traditional nine-to-five shift. Almost any job you can think of is represented in at least one of the armed forces. Job training doesn't just stop once initial training is finished. As service members earn promotions they learn more advanced levels of their jobs. This is because as they move up the ranks, they become responsible for supervising other service members. As enlisted members move up the ranks they become noncommissioned officers (NCOs). NCOs require even more advanced skills. To learn these higher-level skills, they go to schools at several levels along their career. These schools teach leadership along with advanced skills. Officers also go to more schools as they advance in their careers. Service members never stop learning!

Some people start out with one job and then change to another job. Some jobs are not available to brand-new members and take only those with more experience. This is true of most special operations jobs like Navy SEALs and some investigator jobs like criminal investigation division special agent. Soldiers who change jobs don't have to repeat basic training. They just go to the advanced training for their new job. Once they

Coolest Job Ever?

There have been some interesting jobs over the years in the armed forces. From pigeon handlers to artists responsible for painting for the armed forces, citizens have found many ways to serve. During World War II, it was possible to join the Army as a playwright! Some famous people like Stan Lee, creator of the Marvel comic books, and Dr. Seuss got their starts as writers for the Army. Army playwrights were so good that they won three Oscars![1] Of course there are still some pretty cool jobs today. You can even be a hacker![2]

graduate they start their new job. Of course, it is up to the service to decide whether or not to allow members to change to a new job.

Daily Life

Most duty days in the armed forces start with physical training (PT). Each service has its own standards for physical fitness and different routines. While the Army and Air Force sometimes train on swimming, it is very important for sailors specifically to practice swimming. PT usually means lots of push-ups, sit-ups, pull-ups, and running. There are all kinds of interesting exercises that can be used to develop strength and heart fitness. There's even an exercise called the dying cockroach! Some days you get to do something cool like play sports or do an obstacle course for PT. Since service members work different hours, PT is not always in the morning.

After PT, it's off to the dining facility (DFAC), sometimes called the mess hall. For single service members who live on base, they get all of their meals for no charge at military dining facilities. The Navy has dining facilities on its ships. The cooks at these DFACs are usually service members, but sometimes they are civilians. For the cooks, the DFAC is their office. For other members, once they finish their meals, it's off to work. In many cases, the work day starts with a formation. Service members stand in formation to be counted and receive instructions about their tasks for the day.

Because there are so many different jobs in the armed forces, actual workplaces can vary quite a bit. Many service members work out of an office, sitting at a desk with a computer. Sometimes that office, desk, and computer are on the back of a truck in the middle of the desert! Sailors and coasties split their time between land and sea. The Air Force flies a lot, but it takes a lot of people on the ground to make a plane fly. Soldiers and marines spend time in garrison training and go to the field to practice fighting.

Exercises

Members of the armed forces must always remember that their main job is to fight and win wars. Since there is not always a war going on, service members have to find ways to practice. This means that they have to find a way to realistically train. For the Army and Marines, it means going out to the woods or the desert

Physical training (PT) is a crucial part of life in the military.

or even the mountains to practice fighting in different conditions. They never know where they might be called to fight so they have to be prepared. Sailors and coasties have to practice driving ships. The Air Force has to practice flying planes. In every service, there are many members behind the scenes that make those other jobs possible. Would you want to fly in a plane with no mechanic to check it first?

Service members train every single day all over the world. Sometimes the services need to practice larger exercises. These can be big battle simulations where service members pretend to fight each other. It is very important that the different branches of the armed forces can fight together. Several times a year there are large exercises that involve more than just one branch. Sometimes the exercises involve all of the branches. These exercises can last days or even weeks. Training together is the best way to make sure that the services can fight together when it counts. There is an old saying in the Army that says, sweating in training reduces bleeding in war! Of course, it's not always training. In the next chapter, we'll look at what it's like when a service member gets called to serve in faraway lands.

4

Deployment

Every service member knows that they might have to leave their friends and family and go off to serve in foreign lands. This doesn't always mean war. Some service members are stationed in foreign countries. They live and work in most any country you can think of. Of course, sometimes service members have to fight in wars. Other times service members are called upon to save the day in other ways. When there are natural disasters or humanitarian crises around the world, the armed forces are ready and trained to help out. Service members serve all over the world.

Overseas Assignments

Many members of the armed forces live and work in other countries. There are bases in Germany, Korea, Japan, Italy, Spain, and many other countries. Life on these bases is much like life on bases in America. They just happen to be in the middle of another country. One of the biggest challenges is learning a new language. Everything on the base is done in English, but off-base there may be people

The Iraq War, lasting from 2003 to 2011, involved many service members being sent overseas to patrol and sometimes fight.

who do not speak English. Many bases offer language and culture classes to help service members get around their new country.

Navy ships are like big floating bases, and they go all over the world. On these huge ships, you'll find almost anything you would find on any base. They have stores and gyms. They have kitchens and bedrooms. They have libraries and movie rooms. Some are so large they even have swimming pools and running tracks. While they are at sea, Navy ships stop at many foreign ports. Sometimes at these ports the sailors are allowed to go explore the country. At the end of the port call, the sailors all report back to the ship. Then they go back to sailing until they reach the next port or head home.

Members of the armed forces move a lot. Usually, every three years they move to a new base. Sometimes they move after only one year. The armed forces pay for everything for the move. They also help service members by giving them some extra money to get established in their new home. While their basic job stays the same, a new place means a new job with a new team. A computer operator might work for a hospital on one base and then work for a tank company at the next base. Every time they move they get to learn something new.

War

Members of the armed forces can be called on to fight in wars for their country. This might mean fighting at home, but usually it means going somewhere far away. The last time the United States fought here at home was during World War II when

Service members engaged in armed combat with insurgents during the war in Iraq.

Declaring War

War requires an official declaration. Even though he or she commands the military, the president cannot declare war. The US Constitution gives permission to Congress to declare war. The United States has declared war only five times in history.[1] The last time Congress officially declared war was during World War II! The United States has fought in several wars since then, but none of them were official. The wars in Korea, Vietnam, Afghanistan, and Iraq were all fought without a declaration of war. Even without a declaration of war, service members can still be sent to fight.

Japan attacked an island chain.[2] Prior to that, service members on opposite sides fought each other in the American Civil War. It is very unlikely that there will be a need to fight here at home. So, going to war usually means going to another country to fight.

Members of the armed forces must follow orders when those orders are legal. Since the president is the commander in chief of the armed forces, he or she can order service members to go fight. Only Congress can declare war, but service members have been sent lots of places to fight without a declaration of war. When the country decides it has no other option but to fight, members of the armed forces are the ones who do the fighting.

Going to war doesn't always mean fighting. Many service members have been to war and never fired a weapon or been shot at. Eighty percent of all jobs in the military are not combat jobs.[3] Jobs in the armed forces that do most of the actual fighting are called combat arms. These are the infantry, tank drivers, cannon firers, and other jobs where the main job is to fight the enemy. For every one of those fighters, there are four or more support personnel. Of course, even the support personnel can find themselves in danger in war. Sometimes they have to fight, too. That is why every member of the armed forces goes to basic training to learn to fight.

Disaster Relief

Thankfully, there is not always a war going on. Even so, there are events where the help of US service members is necessary. Natural disasters and humanitarian crises can happen anywhere. Hurricanes, earthquakes, tornados, floods, and other natural disasters cause a lot of damage. After a disaster, people can still be in danger because of the conditions left behind. Members of the armed forces have the training to help. No one is better able to get supplies to remote locations or to provide medical care in the harshest conditions.

Sometimes wars between other countries can create problems for the surrounding areas. Refugees and those fleeing from the fight must be cared for. Many countries do not have the resources or the expertise to care for these people. The armed forces can help by providing many services to refugees while protecting them

Members of the US Navy helped evacuate survivors of Hurricane Maria, which hit Puerto Rico in September 2017.

from further harm. Once the members of the armed forces have helped people get their lives back to normal, the service members head home.

Service members are used to making sacrifices for others, like spending time away from their families. Sometimes they are asked to make the ultimate sacrifice. When a member of the armed forces dies or is wounded we owe it to them to recognize their sacrifice. In the next chapter we will look at the sacrifices of service members and their families. We'll also explore how the country honors those who have made those sacrifices. It is up to all of us to make sure that their sacrifices are never forgotten.

5

Making Sacrifices

Members of the armed forces make many sacrifices. They sacrifice their time and comfort and sometimes their lives for a greater cause. Families of service members also make sacrifices. They have to move frequently. They have to be without their loved ones for long periods of time when their service member is deployed. There have been many heroes in the armed forces. The United States honors the sacrifices of members of the armed forces with memorials to their sacrifices. Members of the armed forces make the American way of life possible, but they can pay a heavy price for Americans' freedom.

Families

Members of the armed forces are not the only ones who make sacrifices. Service members have mothers, fathers, brothers, sisters, spouses, and children. When those service members are away their families miss them. Sometimes they don't come home and a family is left to live without them. Even without war, some overseas bases do not allow family members. This means that service members may be away from their family for a year or more at a time. Sometimes families can go for long periods of time without hearing from their loved one.

On top of the hardships of deployments and overseas assignments, family members have their own hardships. Service members usually move every one to three years. Spouses must find new jobs. Children must move to new schools. Everyone must make new friends. It can be very difficult on these families. Being a family member of someone in the armed forces can be challenging, but

Service members often must endure long deployments, separating them from their loved ones.

Family Legacy

Membership in the armed forces can be a family legacy. Harold Hamlin can trace back seven generations of his family that have all served in the armed forces.[1] His father served in World War I. His great great grandfather was in the War of 1812. His great great great grandfather was in the Revolutionary War. Over half of the people who sign up for the armed forces have a parent or other family member who served.[2]

service members could not do what they do without support from their families.

In some families, both parents are in the armed forces. In these cases, grandparents or other family members help care for the children when duty calls. The military tries to keep married couples together, but sometimes they must go to different bases or deploy at different times. While all service members make sacrifices, it can be especially challenging for families where both parents serve.

Heroes

Service in the armed forces can be dangerous. Sometimes service members are killed or wounded. When service members are killed, the country owes them a debt. They died serving their country.

The armed forces have a variety of programs to take care of families who have lost their service member. From life insurance to help moving forward, the armed forces take care of service members' families. Many who serve just want their families to have a better life. It is a comfort to know that even if they are killed, the armed forces will still take care of their family.

Sometimes service members are not killed but they are seriously wounded. The armed forces will take care of wounded service members for the rest of their live. Even so, learning how

Being married to a service member can be challenging, as spouses must often move, changing jobs with each new assignment.

to live with a disability can be very hard. The armed forces provide a wide variety of services to help wounded members live normal lives. From training service dogs, to making replacement limbs, the armed forces work very hard to try and make wounded service members whole again. It is the least that that can be done to take care of those who serve the country.

Memorials

The country honors those who have died in its service. From military cemeteries to monuments, there are special places to honor the fallen. One of the benefits every service member earns is the right to be buried in a military cemetery. Some military cemeteries are hundreds of years old. Veterans of the armed forces can be buried in these special places at no charge to them or their families. On special occasions, people place flags on each of the graves. It is a humbling sight to see, a field of red, white, and blue that reminds us that many have served and many have sacrificed. America's freedom and way of life today is possible because of their service.

There are also many memorials. In Washington, DC, you can find a black granite wall with the names of every service member lost in the Vietnam War. Thousands have made the ultimate sacrifice for their country. We remember them with statues and other monuments as a tribute to their service and sacrifice. These memorials give other citizens a chance to honor those who serve in the armed forces. We cannot forget their service and sacrifice. War is terrible, and we should honor those who face it for us.

Service in the armed forces is a special way for a citizen to help their country. There are many challenges and benefits to service.

Some service members make the ultimate sacrifice for their country, risking and losing their lives to protect America's ideals.

A citizen in the armed forces serves all the other citizens of the country. Because less than 1 percent of Americans will serve in the military, it is an honor that few citizens take upon themselves. They and their families serve and sacrifice for their fellow citizens. They fight so that others can be safe. The next time you see a member of the armed forces make sure you thank them for their service!

CHAPTER NOTES

Chapter 1. United States Armed Forces

1. "Establishment of the Navy," US Navy History and Heritage Command, September 12, 2017, https://www.history.navy.mil/research/library/online-reading-room/title-list-alphabetically/e/establishment-of-the-navy.html.
2. "Status of the Navy," US Navy, October 13, 2017, http://www.navy.mil/navydata/nav_legacy.asp?id=146.
3. "Department of Defense Releases Fiscal Year 2017 President's Budget Proposal," Department of Defense, February 9, 2016, https://www.defense.gov/News/News-Releases/News-Release-View/Article/652687/department-of-defense-dod-releases-fiscal-year-2017-presidents-budget-proposal.
4. "Girl Joins Devil Dogs," *Evening Star*, Washington, DC, August 14, 1918, http://chroniclingamerica.loc.gov/lccn/sn83045462/1918-08-14/ed-1/seq-1/.
5. "Total Force Military Demographics," Department of Defense, http://diversity.defense.gov/LinkClick.aspx?fileticket=gxMVqhkaHh8%3D&.
6. "2015 Demographics," Department of Defense, http://download.militaryonesource.mil/12038/MOS/Reports/2015-Demographics-Report.pdf.

Chapter 2: Joining the Military

1. "Appointment of Temporary Officers in the Army of the United States Upon Mobilization," Department of the Army, December 4, 1987, http://www.apd.army.mil/epubs/DR_pubs/DR_a/pdf/web/r601_50.pdf.

Chapter 3: Serving America

1. Charmain Brackett, "U.S. Army Signal Corps Cherishes Oscar Award," U.S. Army, February 12, 2009, https://www.army.mil/article/16851/us_army_signal_corps_cherishes_oscar_award.
2. "Cyber Operations Specialist," US Army, https://www.goarmy.com/careers-and-jobs/browse-career-and-job-categories/computers-and-technology/cyber-operations-specialist.html.

Chapter 4: Deployment

1. "Official Declarations of War by Congress," United States Senate, https://www.senate.gov/pagelayout/history/h_multi_sections_and_teasers/WarDeclarationsbyCongress.htm.
2. George L. MacGarrigle, "Aleutian Islands," US Army, October 3, 2009, https://history.army.mil/brochures/aleut/aleut.htm.
3. "5 Military Myths—Busted," Military.com, http://www.military.com/join-armed-forces/military-myths.html.

Chapter 5: Making Sacrifices

1. "Legionnaire Counts Seven Generations of U.S. Military Service in His Family Tree," American Legion, March 31, 2014, https://www.legion.org/stories/family-legacy/legionnaire-counts-seven-generations-us-military-service-his-family-tree.
2. V.A. Stander and L.L. Merrill, "The Relationship of Parental Military Background to the Demographic Characteristics of 11,195 Navy Recruits," Naval Health Research Center, April 9, 2000, http://www.dtic.mil/dtic/tr/fulltext/u2/a432135.pdf.

GLOSSARY

active duty To be currently serving in the military.

armed forces The collective name for all of the branches of the military.

coastie Someone who serves in the Coast Guard.

deploy To be sent away from home to provide military service in a foreign country.

draft A process in which citizens were randomly selected and required to serve in the military during times of war.

enlist To join the military.

marine Someone who is in the US Marine Corps.

National Guard A branch of the military that is called up to serve when there are national emergencies.

NCO Noncommissioned officer; an officer who has not received a commission and has risen through the ranks.

officer A leader in the military.

reserves A component of the military that serves part-time and is only called up when more personnel are needed.

ROTC Reserve Officers' Training Corps; an officer training program for college students who are interested in later joining the military.

sailor A member of the Navy.

service member Someone who serves in the military.

soldier Someone who serves in the Army.

special operator A member of the military who has gone through special training and now serves in a special operations force such as the Navy SEALs or Army Rangers.

veteran Someone who used to serve in the military.